THE STORY OF PRINCESS DIANA

A Biography Book for New Readers

—— Written by ——
Jenna Grodzicki

— Illustrated by —
Pearl Law

ROCKRIDGE
PRESS

To my dear friend and educator,
Megan Bennett. You make the world
a better place, one child at a time.

For general information on our other products and services or to obtain technical support, please contact our Customer Care Department within the United States at (866) 744-2665, or outside the United States at (510) 253-0500.

Rockridge Press publishes its books in a variety of electronic and print formats. Some content that appears in print may not be available in electronic books, and vice versa.

TRADEMARKS: Rockridge Press and the Rockridge Press logo are trademarks or registered trademarks of Callisto Media Inc. and/or its affiliates, in the United States and other countries, and may not be used without written permission. All other trademarks are the property of their respective owners. Rockridge Press is not associated with any product or vendor mentioned in this book.

Series Designer: Angela Navarra
Interior and Cover Designer: Rachel Haeseker
Art Producer: Samantha Ulban
Editor: Mary Colgan
Production Editor: Mia Moran
Production Manager: Riley Hoffman

Illustrations © 2021 Pearl Law. Photography © Alamy/PA Images, p.51; Alamy/Trinity Mirrors/Mirrorpix, p.52; Alamy/David Cooper, p.54. Author photo courtesy of Greta Lindquist-Merlino.

Paperback ISBN: 978-1-64876-443-1
eBook ISBN: 978-1-64876-444-8
R0

CONTENTS

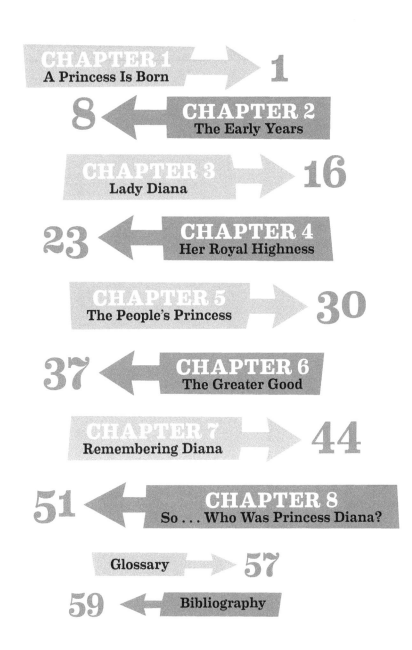

CHAPTER 1

A PRINCESS IS BORN

Meet Princess Diana

As a child, Princess Diana loved animals. She grew up with dogs, rabbits, and hamsters. She had a cat named Marmalade and a Shetland pony named Souffle. Of course, Diana wasn't a princess then. She was Diana Spencer, a kind little girl with a big heart.

Diana was especially proud of her guinea pig, Peanuts. In 1972, she entered Peanuts in a pet show. Peanuts was the winner in the "Fur and Feathers" category. When Diana left for **boarding school**, her beloved Peanuts came with her. While at school, she was made "Head of Pets' Corner."

When Diana grew up, she married Prince

JUMP
—IN THE—
THINK
TANK

Diana wanted to be a ballerina when she grew up. What job would you like to have? Why do you think you'd be good at it?

Charles of England. The young animal lover had once wanted to be a ballerina. Now she was a princess—and one of the most famous women in the world.

Diana used her new role to help people. She visited hospitals to comfort the sick. She was quick to offer a hug or a listening ear. She worked with the homeless to find them shelter and food.

Diana wasn't the first member of the royal family to help people, but she was the first to do so with such kindness and sincerity. She came to be known as the "People's Princess."

Sadly, Diana passed away in a car accident in 1997. She was only 36 years old. In her short time as a princess, she had a big impact on the world. Let's take a closer look at how Diana became a real-life princess and what inspired her to always follow her heart.

❀ **Diana's World** ❀

Diana Frances Spencer was born in Sandringham, England, on July 1, 1961. She had two older sisters, Sarah and Jane. She also had an older brother named John, but Diana never met him. He passed away the same day he was born.

Diana was born into a **wealthy** family. The Spencers were one of England's oldest and most important families. Her parents, John and Frances, held special titles. Diana's family had strong ties to the royal family, too. Her grandmother, Cynthia Spencer, was friends with the queen.

In England, the royal family is made up of the king or queen and their close relatives.

MYTH	&	FACT
The queen of England makes all the laws in the country.		The queen does not make or pass laws. A group of people called **Parliament** is in charge of that.

They are important to the people of the country, but they don't make the laws. In 1953, Queen Elizabeth II was officially crowned queen of England. She is still the queen today.

At that time, the people of England rarely saw the queen in person. They might see her from far away or on TV, but she didn't interact with or speak directly to the people.

Diana's family lived in a fancy house that had its own name. Park House had 10 bedrooms! Outside, there was a swimming pool, a tennis court, and a wide lawn with lots of trees. It was located near Sandringham House, where the royal family sometimes stayed.

When Diana was two years old, her mother gave birth to a baby boy. Her parents named him Charles. The Spencer family was complete.

WHEN?

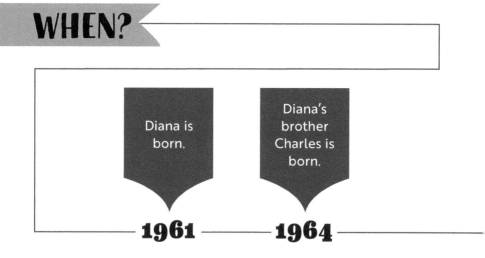

Diana is born.	Diana's brother Charles is born.
1961	**1964**

CHAPTER 2

THE EARLY YEARS

✿ Growing Up ✿

There was never a dull moment at Park House. Diana's sisters were away at boarding school, so her brother became her best friend. They spent a lot of time together. They climbed trees, looked for frogs and newts, and took their dogs for walks. In the summer, Diana  loved to swim in her pool. She dove off the diving board. SPLASH! At night, Diana slept with 20 stuffed animals on her bed. There was hardly any room for her.

Diana and Charles had **nannies** who took care of them. Diana didn't like having a nanny. She wanted to be with her mother. So, the children tried to make the nannies quit. More than once they threw their nannies' clothes out the window!

Despite the tricks she played, Diana was a kind child. She took care of all the family pets. She had many friends, including the queen's younger sons. Sometimes, Prince Andrew and Prince Edward came to swim in their pool. When Diana was five, she played hide-and-seek with Prince Andrew and the queen. Her family often visited the royal family when they were staying at Sandringham House.

Around that same time, Diana's parents decided they didn't want to be married anymore. Her mother moved out of Park House. The children stayed with their father. This made Diana sad. She missed her mother very much. She only saw her on weekends. With her mother gone, Diana often had to take care of Charles.

The Spencer Family

CYNTHIA SPENCER 1897–1972

ALBERT SPENCER 1892–1975

RUTH ROCHE 1908–1993

MAURICE ROCHE 1885–1955

JOHN SPENCER 1924–1992

FRANCES ROCHE SHAND KYDD 1936–2004

SARAH McCORQUODALE 1955–PRESENT

JANE FELLOWES 1957–PRESENT

JOHN SPENCER 1960–1960

DIANA FRANCES SPENCER 1961–1997

CHARLES SPENCER 1964–PRESENT

> **Carry out a random act of seemingly senseless kindness, with no expectation of reward or punishment, safe in the knowledge that one day, someone, somewhere, might do the same for you.**

❀ Off to School ❀

When Diana was nine, she was sent to a boarding school for girls called Riddlesworth Hall. It was two hours away from Park House. Diana didn't want to go. But off she went, with her green stuffed hippo and her guinea pig, Peanuts.

Diana made lots of friends at her new school. She swam and took ballet lessons. In class, she was quiet. She didn't raise her hand or call out answers. However, she won an award for being helpful to others. On weekends and holidays, Diana went back to Park House to be with her family.

When Diana was 12, she joined her older sisters at West Heath School. There, she continued to do well in swimming.

WHERE?

ENGLAND

RIDDLESWORTH HALL

ALTHORP

WEST HEATH

BELGIUM

FRANCE

She shined in her dance lessons. But the classes at this school were hard. Diana had never liked math or science before, and now she felt like she wasn't smart at all.

West Heath encouraged its students to show **good citizenship**. Diana and a friend spent time with an elderly lady who lived near the school. They helped clean her house. Diana also visited patients at a nearby hospital. She made them smile. Diana smiled, too. She felt good when she was helping others.

When Diana was 13, her grandfather passed away. Her father **inherited** Althorp, the Spencer family's mansion in Northamptonshire, England. He also inherited a new title: Earl Spencer. Diana and her sisters and brother got titles, too. She was now Lady Spencer.

JUMP
–IN THE–
THINK TANK

Do you like helping others? What are some things you can do to help your family? Your teachers? Your friends?

The family moved into Althorp. It had 31 bedrooms! Diana missed Park House, but she liked all the open spaces in Althorp. There was plenty of room for her to practice dancing.

WHEN?

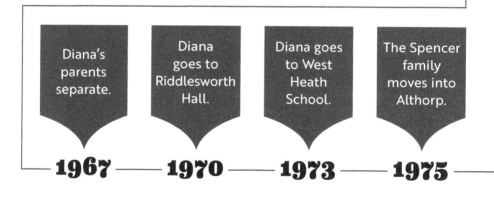

Diana's parents separate.

Diana goes to Riddlesworth Hall.

Diana goes to West Heath School.

The Spencer family moves into Althorp.

1967 — 1970 — 1973 — 1975 —

CHAPTER 3

LADY DIANA

 Fun and Friends

In 1977, Diana's time at West Heath School was almost over. She just had to take her final exams. If she did well, she could go on to college. But Diana did not do well. She failed her final exams. Twice! Diana wasn't upset about this, though. She didn't think college was the right place for her.

Instead, Diana's parents sent her to a finishing school in Switzerland. Finishing schools taught wealthy girls to be proper young ladies.

WHERE?

ENGLAND

LONDON

NETHERLANDS

BELGIUM

GERMANY

FRANCE

SWITZERLAND

INSTITUT ALPIN VIDEMANETTE

They learned things like how to sew, cook, and host parties.

Diana was unhappy at finishing school. She wasn't interested in her lessons. The only thing she liked about her time in Switzerland was learning to ski. Diana wrote letters to her parents, begging them to let her come home. Three months later, they granted her wish.

JUMP
—IN THE—
THINK
TANK

Diana failed her final exams at West Heath. Have you ever failed at anything? What did you do when that happened?

Soon after her return to England, Diana moved to London to stay with her mother and stepfather. She started working as a dance teacher. This was a perfect job for Diana. She enjoyed helping the youngest dancers. Sadly, only a few months later, she hurt her ankle skiing. Her injury ended her dancing career.

When Diana turned 18, her parents bought her an apartment of her own. Her best friends moved in with her. Their home was always

full of laughter. Diana got a job as an assistant teacher at Young England Kindergarten. The children loved her. She played games with them and taught them to dance and draw. On her days off, she babysat for a little boy named Patrick. Diana had never been happier.

✿ Meeting Prince Charles ✿

In the summer of 1980, Diana went to a **polo** match with some friends. Prince Charles was playing. She didn't know it, but her life was about to change forever.

Prince Charles was the oldest son of Queen Elizabeth. Someday, he would be the king of England. His picture was always in the newspapers. Everyone wondered who his future wife would be.

After the polo match, Diana and her friends went to a barbecue. Charles was there, too.

They sat on a hay bale and started talking.

Charles was impressed by Diana's kindness. They talked for hours. At the end of the night, Charles asked Diana if he could see her again. She said yes.

For their first date, Charles took Diana to a musical performance. Then he invited her to a party on the royal **yacht**. More dates followed. Diana visited Charles at one of the royal castles. They went for long walks together. Diana liked spending time with Charles.

Reporters noticed that Charles had a new girlfriend. Soon, Diana's picture was in the newspapers, too. Everyone wanted to know who she was. If the prince liked her, she must be someone special. Reporters waited outside her home and asked her lots of questions. Diana didn't like the attention, but she was always polite.

That winter, Charles went on a skiing trip with some friends. While he was away, he called Diana on the phone. He told her he had something important to ask her when he got home. Diana had a good idea of what his question would be! When Charles returned, he took her to Windsor Castle. He asked her to marry him. Diana said yes!

66 Every single one of us needs to **demonstrate** how much we **care** for our **community**, care for **each other**, and in the process, care **for ourselves.** 99

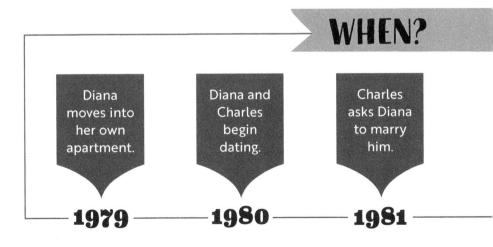

WHEN?

Diana moves into her own apartment.

Diana and Charles begin dating.

Charles asks Diana to marry him.

1979 —— **1980** —— **1981** ——

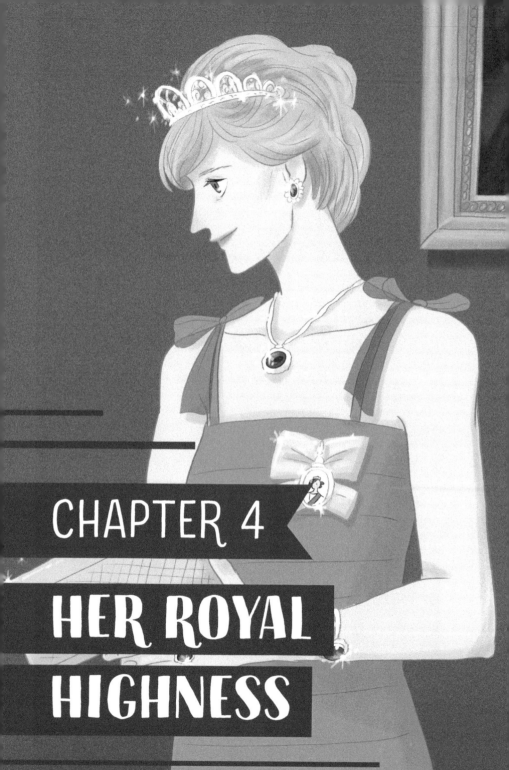

CHAPTER 4

HER ROYAL HIGHNESS

 Palace Life

On February 24, 1981, Charles and Diana shared
the news of their engagement with the world.
They were interviewed on television. Everyone
was excited. Newspapers shared photos of
Diana's engagement ring. It had a sparkly
blue sapphire surrounded by diamonds. Diana
had picked it out herself from a collection of
rings from the crown jeweler. This made some
members of the royal family unhappy. They
thought royals should only wear rings that were
made especially for them.

After the announcement, Diana moved into
Buckingham Palace, the London home of the
royal family. Queen Elizabeth was thrilled! She
thought Diana was a good match for her son.
She sent someone to help Diana get ready for her
duties as a princess. Diana learned the proper
way to sit, bow, and curtsy. She learned how to
wave to a crowd. She was expected to hold her

teacup just so. There was even a rule that said everyone must stop eating when the queen does—even if they're not full!

Life at Buckingham Palace was very busy. In addition to her princess lessons, Diana had a wedding to plan. Still, life at the palace was also lonely. Soon after she arrived, Charles left for a five-week visit to Australia and New Zealand. Diana missed him. She missed her friends, too.

Outside the palace, reporters and photographers followed Diana everywhere. She had become one of the most famous women in the world.

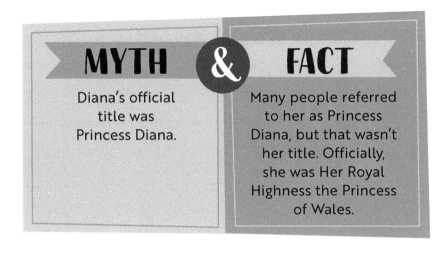

MYTH & FACT

Diana's official title was Princess Diana.

Many people referred to her as Princess Diana, but that wasn't her title. Officially, she was Her Royal Highness the Princess of Wales.

It seemed like everyone wanted to know what she was doing every second of every day. This made Diana uncomfortable, but she tried her best to keep smiling.

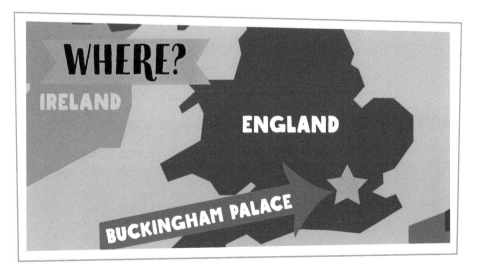

WHERE?

IRELAND

ENGLAND

BUCKINGHAM PALACE

✿ The Royal Wedding ✿

On the morning of July 29, 1981, Diana woke up early. She felt both excited and nervous. It was her wedding day! And the whole world would be watching.

Diana put on her wedding dress. Made with sequins, lace, and 10,000 pearls, Diana's silk wedding dress is one of the most famous dresses in history. It had puffy sleeves and a 25-foot-long train that trailed behind as she walked. She wore the Spencer family tiara on her head.

Diana and her father rode in a horse-drawn glass carriage to St. Paul's Cathedral. Thousands of people lined the streets, hoping to see Diana. They cheered and waved, and Diana waved back. Around 750 million people from all over the world watched the wedding on TV.

After the ceremony, the bride and groom rode in an open carriage to Buckingham Palace.

They stood on the balcony and waved at the
crowd below. Then they went inside for a
special wedding breakfast with 120 guests.
Their wedding cake was five feet tall and
weighed 255 pounds!

Diana and Charles left for their honeymoon
later that day. They went on a cruise around the
Mediterranean aboard the royal yacht. Diana
hoped she and Charles would finally have some
time to themselves. But the yacht had a crew of

JUMP
—IN THE—
THINK TANK

Millions of people watched Diana and Charles's wedding. Why do you think that is? Why did all of those people care about it?

more than 200 sailors. Diana and Charles were rarely alone. This wasn't the honeymoon she had hoped for. Diana, now Her Royal Highness the Princess of Wales, was beginning to see that life as a royal was not like a fairy tale.

WHEN?

Diana and Charles announce their engagement.

FEB 24 1981

Diana and Charles are married.

JUL 29 1981

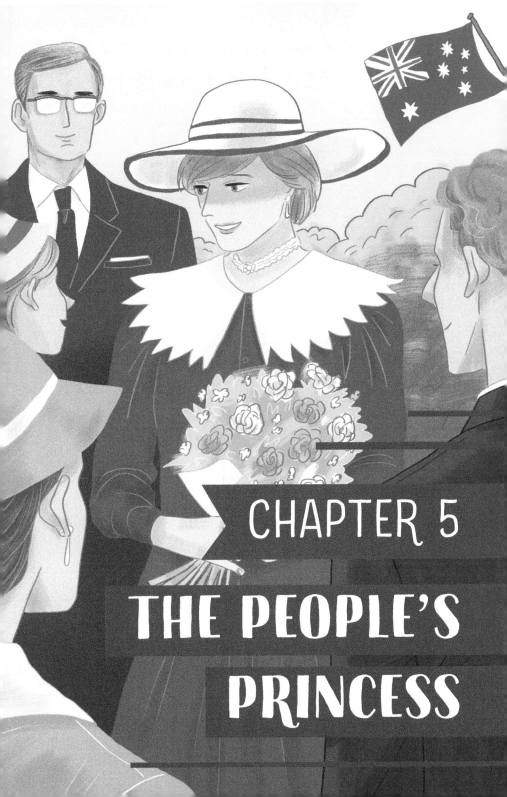

CHAPTER 5
THE PEOPLE'S PRINCESS

❀ A New Role ❀

As a new member of the royal family, Diana
had many duties to fulfill. She attended
fancy dinners and garden parties and gave
speeches to large crowds. Diana was also
busy decorating her two homes. She and
Charles divided their time between Highgrove
House in the country and Kensington Palace
in London.

In October 1981, Diana learned she was going
to have a baby. Both she and Charles were
thrilled. Prince William Arthur Philip Louis
was born on June 21, 1982. People everywhere
celebrated the birth of the future king. Diana
and Charles spent the next several months at
home, caring for their new baby.

In 1983, Diana and Charles visited Australia
and New Zealand for six weeks. They took
baby William with them. Diana charmed
everyone she met. She smiled, shook hands,

and spoke directly to the people. She knelt on the ground to look children in the eyes. This was something new. In the past, royals waved but kept their distance. Diana made people feel like she truly cared about them. They loved her for it.

Despite all the smiles she shared in public, Diana was unhappy in her marriage. She and Charles had different interests, and they began to grow apart. William was the bright spot in Diana's life, and she was overjoyed when she found out a second baby was on the way.

JUMP
—IN THE—
THINK
TANK

Why do you think Diana wanted her children to have a "normal" childhood?

Prince Henry Charles Albert David was born on September 15, 1984. They called him Harry. Diana loved being a mother. Even though her boys had nannies, she spent as much time as possible with them. She wanted William and Harry to know they were loved.

Diana was also determined to give her sons a "normal" childhood. She took them to the beach and played in the sand with them. She brought them places royals didn't usually go, like amusement parks and McDonald's.

❀ A Helping Hand ❀

Diana had always enjoyed helping others. Now she wanted to set a good example for her sons. Diana began to **volunteer** with several different **charities**. A charity is a group that helps people who are poor, sick, or in need.

WHERE?

ENGLAND

AUSTRALIA

NEW ZEALAND

KENSINGTON PALACE

HIGHGROVE HOUSE

In 1987, Diana opened a new wing of a London hospital that would treat AIDS patients. Many people were afraid to get close to people who had AIDS, which is a serious disease—but Diana wasn't. A photographer snapped a picture of her shaking hands with an AIDS patient. That photo was shared in newspapers and magazines all over the world. People were impressed with Diana's **compassion**.

Diana made it her royal mission to help people who were suffering. She traveled to countries with high rates of a disease called leprosy to spread awareness of this illness. She spent time with children in orphanages and visited hospitals to comfort children with cancer. She supported charities that worked to give homeless teens a better future. Her work inspired others to help, too.

Diana became president or **patron** to more than 100 charities as part of her royal duties. In 1989, she took a trip to New York City, where she visited

a homeless shelter for families. Diana spent time with the people there and listened to their stories. She sat in the bedroom of one little boy and chatted about his poster of the popular basketball player Michael Jordan.

In 1992, Diana met one of her role models, Mother Teresa. Mother Teresa was a nun who devoted her life to helping the poorest of the poor in India. She was 82 years old. Despite their difference in age, the two formed a friendship. They shared a passion for bringing love to the needy.

 Anywhere I see suffering, that is where I want to be, doing what I can.

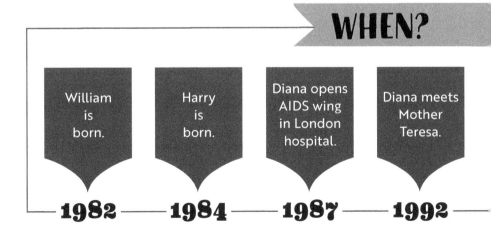

WHEN?

| William is born. | Harry is born. | Diana opens AIDS wing in London hospital. | Diana meets Mother Teresa. |
| 1982 | 1984 | 1987 | 1992 |

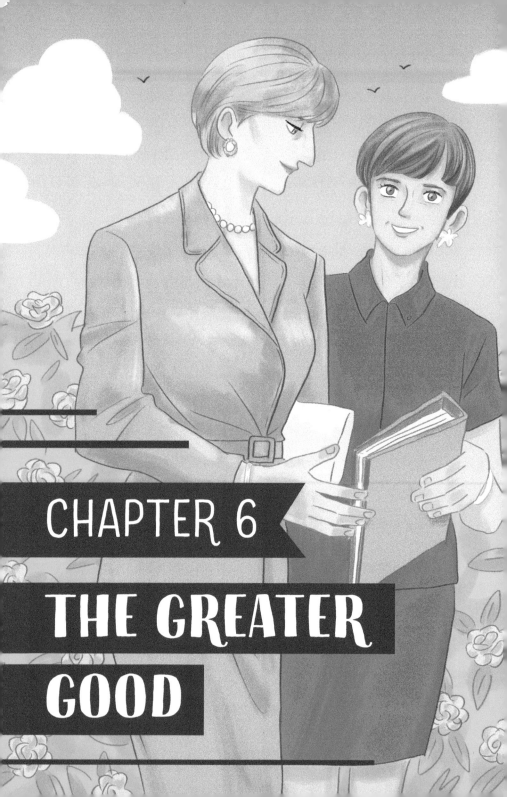

CHAPTER 6

THE GREATER GOOD

❀ A New Start ❀

Diana continued to find happiness in her charity work, but she did not have that same happiness in her marriage. By 1992, Diana and Charles were spending most of their time apart. He was busy with traveling and his royal duties. She was busy visiting hospitals and raising money for her charities.

Eventually, they decided to separate. Diana would live at Kensington Palace, and Charles would live at Highgrove House. Their love for each other may have faded, but they both fiercely loved their sons. William and Harry were away at boarding school, but on the weekends and holidays, their time would be split between their parents.

Diana was sad that she would have less time with her boys. Still, she was hopeful for a happier future. She was still expected to attend some royal events with Charles, but she was released from her official royal duties.

In 1996, Diana and Charles **divorced**. Their marriage was officially over. Diana's title changed, too. She was no longer Her Royal Highness. She was now Diana, Princess of Wales. She continued to live in Kensington Palace, and the boys continued to spend equal time with their parents.

Even though she was no longer the wife of the future king, Diana remained one of the

most famous women in the world. Over the years, she had become close with many famous fashion designers. They designed clothes especially for her. She was a style **icon**. People still wanted to see the beautiful dresses Diana was wearing. And they still wanted to know what she was doing. Reporters and photographers still followed her all the time.

✿ Changing the World ✿

Before the divorce in 1996, Diana stepped down as patron to most of her charities. Many were connected to her royal duties, which she no longer had. Diana still wished to help people, though. She continued to support the causes that were most important to her. These included AIDS, cancer, leprosy, children's hospitals, and homelessness. She also supported ballet, one of her childhood passions. She raised money for the English National Ballet.

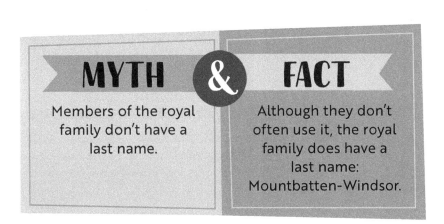

MYTH & FACT

Members of the royal family don't have a last name.

Although they don't often use it, the royal family does have a last name: Mountbatten-Windsor.

Diana often spoke with her sons about how **privileged** they were. She wanted them to recognize the importance of helping those in need. Diana brought William and Harry with her to visit hospitals and homeless shelters. She hoped they would one day follow in her footsteps.

In 1997, Diana took a trip to Angola, a country in southern Africa. She wanted to help survivors of **land mines**. Land mines are small bombs that are buried just under the ground.

They explode when people or vehicles go by. They are used during times of war. After the wars are over, many land mines stay in the ground, forgotten. Innocent people may step on them and get hurt or killed.

Diana met children who were land mine survivors. She walked across minefields. Her visit was reported all over the world. She made people everywhere see what a huge problem land mines are. Diana's visit helped build support for a worldwide **ban** on land mines.

JUMP
−IN THE−
THINK TANK

Diana helped many charities that supported causes that were important to her. What causes are important to you?

Inspired by his mother's important work, 14-year-old William suggested that Diana **auction** off some of her fancy gowns and give the money to charity. So, in June 1997, 79 of Diana's dresses went up for auction. In total, the event raised over $3 million! The money was donated to AIDS and cancer charities.

WHEN?

Diana and Charles separate.	Diana and Charles divorce.	Diana visits Angola.	Diana auctions off her dresses for charity.
1992	**1996**	**1997**	**1997**

CHAPTER 7
REMEMBERING DIANA

✿ The World's Loss ✿

Photographers continued to follow Diana wherever she went. They hid behind bushes to try to get the best shot. They chased after her car and snapped pictures of her through the window. Newspapers and magazines paid a lot of money for these pictures. One photograph of Diana even sold for $6 million!

On the evening of August 30, 1997, Diana was eating dinner with a friend at a fancy hotel in Paris. A large group of photographers waited outside. Diana didn't want her picture taken. She left the hotel through a back door and got in her car. Her driver sped away, but the photographers noticed. They raced after Diana on motorcycles and in cars.

All the vehicles were going too fast. Diana's driver lost control, and her car crashed. Diana didn't survive the accident. She was only 36 years old.

News of Diana's death shocked the world. Everyone **mourned** the loss of this caring and compassionate woman. To show their love and support, people left flowers all over London. In total, 60 million flowers were left in **honor** of Diana! There were so many outside Diana's Kensington Palace home, it looked like the ground was covered by a giant blanket.

Diana's **funeral** was held on September 6, 1997. Crowds gathered on the streets and outside the church. Sarah, Jane, and Charles Spencer each spoke of their love for their sister. A famous singer sang a song he wrote to honor Diana. More than 2.5 billion people around the world watched the funeral on television.

Later that day, Diana was buried on a small island in the middle of a lake at Althorp.

Soon after Diana's death, the Diana, Princess of Wales Memorial Fund was created. People donated money to it. That money went to the charities that were most important to Diana.

✺ Diana's Legacy ✺

Today, Diana's **legacy** lives on in her children. Just as she hoped, William and Harry grew up and followed their mother's example.

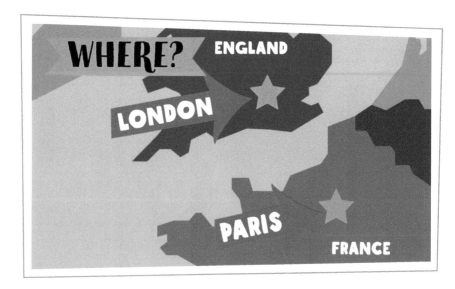

WHERE? ENGLAND
LONDON
PARIS
FRANCE

They continue to support the charities Diana cared about. They have also found other ways to help. William has raised money to protect animals and the environment. Harry has worked hard to support **veterans** and orphans in Africa. Together, both princes have worked with charities that provide help for people with **mental health** problems.

JUMP
–IN THE–
THINK
TANK

People who had never even met Diana were so sad when she died. Why do you think that is?

William and Harry each have families of their own now. William is married to Catherine "Kate" Middleton. She is called the Duchess of Cambridge. When William asked her to marry him, he gave Kate his mother's blue sapphire and diamond ring. They have three children, Prince George, Princess Charlotte, and Prince Louis.

Harry is married to Meghan Markle. She is called the Duchess of Sussex. Meghan's engagement ring also honors Diana. It has two stones that were part of Diana's jewelry collection. Harry and Meghan have two children, Archie and Lilibet. They gave Lilibet a special middle name: Diana!

William and Harry work hard to keep their mother's memory alive. They had a royal statue made of her. It is located in the gardens at Kensington Palace. The statue was **unveiled** on July 1, 2021. That would have been Diana's 60th birthday. William and Harry hope people will visit the statue and remember their mother.

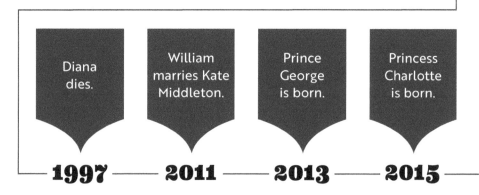

WHEN?

Diana dies.	William marries Kate Middleton.	Prince George is born.	Princess Charlotte is born.
1997	**2011**	**2013**	**2015**

In her short time here, Diana made the world a better place. She showed everyone what true kindness looks like. She helped so many people. And she inspired others to help those in need, too. She will always be remembered as the People's Princess.

> ❝ I knew what my job was; it was to go out and meet the people and love them. ❞

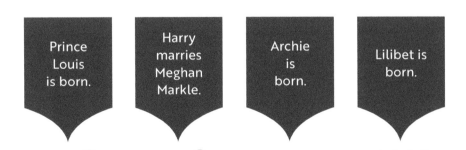

Prince Louis is born.	Harry marries Meghan Markle.	Archie is born.	Lilibet is born.
2018	2018	2019	2021

CHAPTER 8

SO . . . WHO WAS PRINCESS DIANA?

🌸 Challenge Accepted! 🌸

Now that you've learned all about Princess Diana, let's test your new knowledge in a little who, what, when, where, why, and how quiz. Feel free to look back in the text to find the answers if you need to, but try to remember first!

1 **Where was Diana born?**
> A   Paris, France
> B   London, England
> C   New York City
> D   Sandringham, England

2 **Who was Diana's best friend when she was growing up?**
> A   Jane, her sister
> B   Sarah, her sister
> C   Charles, her brother
> D   Peanuts, her guinea pig

3 What did Diana win an award
for at Riddlesworth Hall?

→ A   Being helpful

→ B   Winning a race

→ C   Baking a cake

→ D   Swimming

4 Which job did Diana have before
she married Prince Charles?

→ A   Secretary

→ B   Ballerina

→ C   Assistant teacher

→ D   Nurse

5 How many people watched Diana
and Charles's wedding on TV?

→ A   750

→ B   750,000

→ C   750 million

→ D   750 billion

6 **What are Diana's sons' names?**
(Hint: There is more than one answer.)

→ A   George

→ B   Harry

→ C   Archie

→ D   William

7 **Why did people all over the world care about Diana?**

→ A   She was married to the future king.

→ B   She was a style icon.

→ C   She worked with lots of charities.

→ D   All of the above.

8 **What did Diana sell at an auction to raise money for charities?**

→ A   Her jewelry

→ B   Her dresses

→ C   Her shoes

→ D   Her purses

9   What was Diana known as?

→ A   The Fashion Princess

→ B   The Kind Princess

→ C   The Park House Princess

→ D   The People's Princess

10   What are some ways Diana tried to make the world a better place?

→ A   She raised money to help homeless people.

→ B   She worked to get a worldwide ban on land mines.

→ C   She visited hospitals to comfort children with cancer.

→ D   All of the above.

 Our World

Princess Diana made a difference in the lives of people all over the world. Let's take a look at some of the ways Diana's work is still having an impact today.

→ Diana changed the way the public felt about people with AIDS. When she shook the hand of the AIDS patient in the London hospital, she was the first to show the world that the virus couldn't be spread by touch.

→ The Diana, Princess of Wales Memorial Fund continued to raise money long after her death. This gave supporters the opportunity to carry on Diana's legacy and ensure the charities she cared about would not be forgotten.

→ Diana's work with land mine survivors in Angola helped lead to a successful ban on land mines. Many countries have now made it illegal to create and use land mines. Prince Harry continues to support this work today.

JUMP
—IN THE—
THINK
TANK
FOR

MORE!

Now let's think a little bit more about Diana's life and how her work changed the world.

→ How did being a member of the royal family help Diana succeed in her charity work? Do you think she would have made as big of a difference if she wasn't a princess?

→ Throughout her life, Diana didn't let fear stop her from doing what she thought was right. What are some examples of times Diana showed bravery? When have you shown bravery?

→ Diana has been called the People's Princess. Why is that a good name for her?

Glossary

auction: A public sale at which things are sold to the people who offer the most money

ban: A law that makes something illegal

boarding school: A place where students live and study, staying away from home

charities: Groups that help people in need

compassion: A feeling of sharing another's suffering that leads to a desire to help

divorce: The legal ending of a marriage between two people

funeral: A ceremony for someone who has died

good citizenship: Doing your best to make your community a better place

honor: To show respect for a person, place, or thing

icon: A person who is greatly respected or admired

inherit: To receive something from a person who has died

land mines: Small bombs that are buried just under the ground

legacy: Something a person leaves behind for which they are remembered

mental health: The well-being of a person's mind and emotions

mourn: To feel or act very sad because of a death or great loss

nannies: People who are hired to take care of other people's children

Parliament: A group of people who make the laws for the country

patron: A person who gives money or other support to a group or a cause

polo: A game played on horseback by two teams of three or four members each. The players use mallets with long handles to hit a small wooden ball into the other team's goal.

privileged: Having special rights or opportunities only granted to certain people instead of everyone

unveiled: Displayed or shared for the first time

veterans: People who have served in the armed forces

volunteer: To spend time working for a cause without being paid

wealthy: Having plenty or being rich

yacht: A type of boat that is used for recreation

Bibliography

Bashir, Martin. "An Interview with HRH the Princess of Wales." *Panorama*. Aired November 20, 1995, on BBC1, London.

Brown, Tina. *The Diana Chronicles*. New York: Doubleday, 2007.

Clayton, Tim, and Phil Craig. *Diana: Story of a Princess*. New York: Pocket Books, 2001.

Jennings, Tom, and David Tillman, dir. *Diana: In Her Own Words*. Beverly Hills, CA: Twentieth Century Fox, 2017.

Labrecque, Ellen. *Who Was Princess Diana?* New York: Penguin Workshop, 2017.

Mattern, Joanne. *Princess Diana (DK Biography)*. New York: DK Publishing, Inc., 2006.

Morton, Andrew. *Diana: Her True Story*. Rev. ed. New York: Simon & Schuster, 1997.

Royal.uk. Accessed March 1, 2021.

Acknowledgments

I remember the exact moment I learned of Princess Diana's death. I was moving into my dorm for my freshman year at Boston College. While I knew it was a tragic loss for the entire world, I didn't truly understand the impact she had made until I began the research for this book. I'm honored I was given the opportunity to share Princess Diana's story with young readers. I'd like to thank my editor, Mary Colgan, for believing in my writing and helping to make it shine. Big thanks to my husband, Shawn, and my children, Tessa and Tanner, for their love and support. I hope children will be inspired by Princess Diana to be kind, follow their hearts, and always help those in need.

About the Author

JENNA GRODZICKI is the author of many fiction and nonfiction children's books. Her books include *I See Sea Food: Sea Creatures That Look Like Food* and *Harmony Humbolt: The Perfect Pets Queen*. Jenna lives near the beach with her husband, two kids, two cats, and one dog. She spent more than 10 years as an educator, but now she's a full-time writer. Jenna loves to read and go skiing with her family. To learn more, visit her website at JennaGrodzicki.com.

About the Illustrator

PEARL LAW is an illustrator, zine-maker, comic artist, and visual recorder. She loves to play around with visual wit and exploring the best narrative possible through problem-solving, solid line work, and nice bold colors. Much of her work takes inspiration from humor, literature, history, and behavioral observations. Pearl graduated from University of the West of England in the UK with a degree in illustration. She now lives in Hong Kong and fantasizes about living in a cottage someday.

WHO WILL INSPIRE YOU NEXT?

EXPLORE A WORLD OF HEROES AND ROLE MODELS IN
THE STORY OF... BIOGRAPHY SERIES FOR NEW READERS.

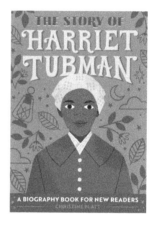
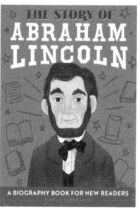

LOOK FOR THIS SERIES
WHEREVER BOOKS AND EBOOKS ARE SOLD

Alexander Hamilton

Albert Einstein

Martin Luther King Jr.

George Washington

Jane Goodall

Barack Obama

Helen Keller

Marie Curie